Ancho and Poblano Chiles

Additional Terra Nova Books in
The Pepper Pantry Series by Dave DeWitt:

The Essential Chile Sauce Guide
The Essential Hot Spice Guide
Jalapeños
New Mexican Chiles
Sweet Heat

THE PEPPER PANTRY
Ancho and Poblano Chiles

Dave DeWitt, *the Pope of Peppers*

Terra Nova Books
SANTA FE, NEW MEXICO

Library of Congress Control Number 2016958551

Distributed by SCB Distributors, (800) 729-6423

Terra Nova Books

Ancho and Poblano Chiles. Copyright © 2012 by Dave DeWitt
Second edition published 2017 by Terra Nova Books
Printed in the United States of America

Published by Terra Nova Books, Santa Fe, New Mexico.
www.TerraNovaBooks.com

ISBN 978-1-938288-29-6

Contents

The Legacy of the Aztecs

n 1529, Bernardino de Sahagún, a Spanish Franciscan friar living in *Nueva España* (Mexico) noted that the Aztecs ate hot red or yellow chile peppers in their hot chocolate—and in nearly every other dish they prepared as well! Fascinated by the Aztecs' constant use of a previously unknown spice, Sahagún documented this fiery cuisine in his classic study, *Historia General de las Cosas de la Nueva España,* now known as the Florentine Codex. His work indicates that of all the pre-Columbian New World civilizations, it was the Aztecs who loved chile peppers the most.

The marketplaces of ancient Mexico overflowed with chile peppers of all sizes and shapes, and Sahagún wrote that they included "hot green chiles, smoked chiles, water chiles, tree chiles, beetle chiles, and sharp-pointed red chiles." In addition to some twenty varieties of *chillis,* as the pungent pods were called in the Nahuatl language, vendors sold strings of red chiles (modern *ristras*), precooked chiles, and "fish chiles," which were the earliest known forms of ceviche, a dish for which fish is preserved without cooking in a marinade of an acidic fruit juice and chile peppers. Based on the friar's descriptions, there is no doubt that early forms of the ancho/poblano variety were in the Aztec markets.

Father Sahagún, one of the first behavioral scientists, also noted that chiles were revered as much as sex by the ancient Aztecs. While fasting to appease their rather bloodthirsty gods, the priests required two abstentions by the faithful: sexual relations and chile peppers.

Aztec cookery was the basis for the Mexican food of today, and, in fact, many Aztec dishes have lasted through the centuries virtually unchanged. Since oil and fat were not generally used in Aztec cooking, the foods were usually roasted, boiled, or cooked in sauces. The sauce legacy especially lives on today, as we will see.

PART 1

The Chile of the People and the Wide One

NOMENCLATURE

The fresh green form is called *chile poblano,* or "chile of the people," and "poblano" is descriptive of the Valley of Puebla, where large-scale production may have first begun. Literally, *chile ancho* means "wide chile pepper," an allusion to the broad, flat, heart-shaped dried pod that results from sun-drying of the mature red poblano pod. In the United States, the variety is called "ancho/poblano," but in Mexico, the variety is called "ancho," and the poblano is its processed green form. In Baja California, both the green and dried pods are called "ancho." Further adding to the confusion are the terms *mulato* ("light brown") and *negro* ("black"), which refer to varieties of the Mexican ancho. In California, the confusion increases because poblanos are called "pasillas" by the produce industry.

HORTICULTURAL HISTORY

The earliest poblano forms were probably cultivated in pre-Columbian times, and the present varieties are at least a century old, attesting to their popularity in the cooking of Mexico. About thirty-seven thousand acres are under cultivation in Mexico, particularly in the dry valleys of central Mexico in the states of Guanajuato, San Luis Potosi, Durango, Zacatecas, and Aguascalientes. They are also grown to a lesser extent in the coastal regions of the states of Sinaloa, Coahuila, and Nayarit. Popular Mexican varieties of the ancho are "Esmeralda," "Verdeno," and "Flor de Pabellon"; the mulato variety is represented by "V-2" and "Roque."

Legend and Lore

> Chile, they say, is the king, the soul of the Mexicans,
> A nutrient, a medicine, a drug, a comfort.
> For many Mexicans, if it were not for the existence of
>   chile,
> Their national identity would begin to disappear.
> —from *El Chile y Otros Picantes*, by Arturo Lomeli

The Ancho chile figures prominently in the legend of the origin of the famous Mexican dish *mole poblano*. The story goes that the dish was invented in the sixteenth century by Sor Andrea de la Asuncíon, a Dominican nun at the convent of Santa Rosa in the city of Puebla. It seems that the archbishop was coming to visit, and the nuns were worried because they had no food elegant enough to serve someone of his eminence. So they prayed for guidance, and one of the nuns had a vision. She directed that everyone in the convent begin chopping and grinding everything edible they could find in the kitchen. Into a pot went chiles, tomatoes, nuts, sugar, tortillas, bananas, raisins, garlic, avocados, and dozens of herbs and spices. The final ingredient was the magic one: chocolate. Then the nuns slaughtered their only turkey and cooked and served it with the mole sauce over it to the archbishop, who declared it the finest dish he had ever tasted.

It's a nice story, but a more likely scenario suggests that mole poblano was invented by the Aztecs long before the Spaniards arrived. Since chocolate was reserved for Aztec royalty, the military nobility, and religious officials, perhaps Aztec serving girls at the convent gave a royal recipe to the nuns so they could honor their own royalty, the archbishop. At any rate, the recipe for mole poblano was rescued from oblivion and became a holiday favorite. Our recipe for Classic Mole Poblano Sauce should be considered a basis for experimentation, including with the ingredients mentioned above.

PART 2

From Seed to Shelf

Botanical Description and Heat Scale

This chile is a pod type of the annuum species. The fresh poblano plants are multiple-stemmed and compact to semi-erect, semi-woody, and about twenty-five inches high. The leaves are dark green and shiny, approximately four inches long and two and a half inches wide, and the corollas are off-white and appear at every node. The flowering period begins fifty days after sowing and continues until the first frost. The pods are pendant, vary from three to six inches long and two to four inches wide, are conical or truncated, and have indented shoulders. Immature pods are dark green, maturing to either red or brown, and the dried pods are a very dark reddish-brown, sometimes nearly black. Ancho/poblanos are a relatively mild chile, varying between 1,000 and 1,500 Scoville Heat Units.

Agriculture

This variety is one of the most popular peppers grown in Mexico, where about thirty-seven thousand acres of it are under cultivation. The ancho/poblano varieties grow well in the U.S., but only about a hundred fifty acres are planted. Growers in the eastern U.S. have reported that plants grown in Wharton, New Jersey, topped four feet and needed to be staked to keep them from toppling over. These plants produced well, but the pods never matured to the red stage before the end of the growing season. The usual growing period is a hundred to a hundred twenty days, and the yield is about fifteen pods per plant, although there are reports of up to thirty pods per plant.

RECOMMENDED ANCHO/POBLANO VARIETIES

"Ancho 101" is a mild variety three to four inches long by two to three inches wide with medium-thick flesh. It matures from dark green to red with plants thirty to thirty-six inches high and pendant pods that ripen in mid-season. They are stuffed when fresh and used in mole sauces when dried.

"Ancho 211 Hybrid" has medium heat with pods four to five inches long by two to two and a half inches wide, with medium thick flesh. The plants are twenty-four to thirty inches tall, and the pods mature from dark green to red in mid-season. The pods are stuffed when green or fresh red; the dried anchos are ground into powders and used in mole sauces.

"Ancho Gigantia" is a mild variety with pods four to six inches long by two and a half to three inches wide, with medium-thick flesh. The plants are thirty-six to forty-two inches tall, and the pods are pendant, maturing from dark green to red in mid-season. Like the others, the fresh pods are stuffed, and the dried ancho pods are ground into powder and used in mole sauces.

"Ancho Mulato" is a mild variety with pods three to five inches long by two to two and a half inches wide, with medium- thick flesh. The plants are thirty-six to forty-two inches tall, and the pods are pendant, ripening in mid-season when they turn from dark green to brownish-red. In cooking, the pods are used the same way as above.

"Tiburon Hybrid" has medium heat, and that could be the reason the variety is named "shark"—it bites you. The pods are large, five to seven inches long by two and a half to three and a half inches wide, with medium-thick flesh. The plants grow from twenty-four to thirty inches tall, maturing from green to red in mid-season. Culinary uses are the same as above.

POBLANO GARDENING TIPS

Seeds to Seedlings

About six weeks before the time to transplant seedlings into the garden, I start the seeds in plastic six-pack seedling growers, just like commercial greenhouses. I use a vermiculite-based growing medium rather than soil because the seedlings' roots receive more oxygen and thus grow faster.

The six packs are set in trays on top of heating wire or tape to keep soil temperatures above seventy-five degrees, since the warmth of the soil can radically affect the germination percentage of most chile varieties.

The seedlings should be grown in full sun in a greenhouse or window so they do not become "leggy" and topple over. Some leggy seedlings may be pinched back to make a bushier plant and ensure that leaf growth does not overwhelm stem growth. Keep the seedlings moist but not wet; overwatering will cause stem rot. It will also be necessary to fertilize the plants after they have put out their first true leaves. I use an all-purpose, water-soluble fertilizer (15-30-15), one-quarter teaspoon to a gallon of water, every time I water my seedlings. When growing seedlings in the house, remember that cats love to graze on tender young plants, which will not harm the cats but will destroy the chiles.

Planting the Poblanos

Chile peppers should not be set out in the garden until after the last frost, and ideally should not be set out until the temperature of the garden soil four inches below the surface reaches sixty-five degrees. Before transplanting, the seedlings should be "hardened off" by placing the trays outside for a few hours each day during warm, sunny days. Constant movement of the seedlings from light breezes will strengthen the stems and prepare the plants for the rigors of the garden. Chile pepper gardeners living in particularly chilly regions should wait until the plants blossom before planting them in the garden.

If the garden plot is to be irrigated, use a shovel to make rows and furrows, and then set the chile pepper plants one to two feet apart. Though more plants could be crammed into the garden, or the square footage reduced, this size and spacing works best for me mainly because it lets me harvest the pods without stomping on the plants. Some gardeners place the chiles as close as eight inches apart so the plants will shade each other and protect the fruit from sunburn. If necessary, protect the young chile plants from freak frosts and cutworms by covering them with glass or plastic jars at night.

After transplanting the chiles, the garden should be thoroughly mulched. Use several layers of newspaper in hot climates or black plastic film in cool summer climates. Where summer temperatures regularly are in the nineties, black plastic in a garden can raise the temperature in that micro-climate so high that the plants will stop flowering. Layers of newspaper weighted down with soil reflect sunlight, hold water, and provide additional organic material for the soil after they disintegrate.

The Growing Season

Chiles need regular water and plenty of it, but overwatering is the biggest mistake of the home gardener. Well-drained soil is the key here, and the first indication of overwatering is water standing in the garden for any length of time. Some wilting of the plants in the hot summer sun is normal and does not always mean the plants need water.

In a well-managed garden with abundant added organic material such as compost, no further fertilizing will be necessary.

To set fruit, the plants require daytime temperatures between sixty-five and eighty degrees and night temperatures above fifty-five degrees. Flowering decreases during the hottest months of the summer, and, in fact, extremely hot or dry conditions will result in the blossoms' dropping off the plant. However, in the early fall, flowering picks up again, though in northern regions, fall blooms are unlikely to yield fruit. In most locations, the first hard frost will kill the plants, and the remaining pods then should be removed.

Quite a few obnoxious pests and diseases can attack poblano chile plants, but I have been lucky. My most serious problem was an aphid attack on the seedlings in the greenhouse. Poblanos are also attacked by wilt disease, which is promoted by overly wet soil. Always remove and destroy all diseased plants.

Chile plants and pods are assaulted by a large number of insect pests, including aphids, beetles, borers, bugs, flies, hoppers, miners, mites, scales, and worms. Interestingly enough, chiles can protect themselves if you transform the hottest pods available into an organic insecticide. Take eight ounces of the hottest pods in the garden and liquefy them in a blender with a small onion, six cloves of garlic, one tablespoon of natural soap, three tablespoons of pyrethrum powder, and two or more cups of water. Strain the mixture through cheese cloth and dilute with water to the desired consistency for use in a sprayer. Spray the tops and bottoms of the pepper leaves every forty-eight hours, and most insect pests will be deterred though not killed.

Harvesting the Heat

The poblanos can be eaten or processed as soon as they are about four inches long, or they can be allowed to turn red before picking and drying. However, it is important to continue harvesting the ripe pods as they mature. If the pods are allowed to remain on the plant, few new ones will form, whereas if the pods are continually harvested, the plants will produce great numbers of pods. The best time to pick chiles for drying is when they first start to turn red. This timing will stimulate the plant into further production, and the harvested chiles can be strung to dry and will turn bright red. When harvesting, it is best to cut the peppers off the plants with a knife or scissors because the branches are brittle and will often break before the stem of the chile pod will.

Preserving the Pods

Roasting and Peeling the Poblanos

The poblano varieties need to be blistered and peeled before being used. Blistering or roasting the chile is the process of heating it to the point that the tough transparent skin is separated from the meat of the chile so it can be removed. Chile pepper grower Stuart Hutson of Mesilla, New Mexico, describes this process as: "Roasting the hides off them but not cooking them." While processing the chile, be sure to wear rubber gloves to protect yourself from the capsaicin that can burn your hands and any other part of your body that you touch. Before roasting, cut a small slit in the chile near the top so the steam can escape. The chiles can then be placed on a baking sheet and put directly under the broiler, or on a screen on the top of the stove.

My favorite method, which involves meditation with a six-pack of dark beer, is to place the pods on a charcoal grill about five to six inches from the coals. Blisters will soon indicate that the skin is separating, but be sure that the chiles are blistered—even blackened slightly—all over, or they will not peel properly. Immediately wrap the chiles in damp towels or place them in a plastic bag for ten to fifteen minutes—this "steams" them and loosens the skins. For crisper, less-cooked chile, plunge them into ice water to stop the cooking process. The idea is to use intense heat for short periods of time rather than low heat for a long time. During the grill-roasting process, the sugar and starch caramelize in the chile, which imparts a cooked flavor, while a rapid roasting over high heat leaves the chile tasting more raw. And, during the roasting process, why not save a few perfectly formed pods and make a classic dish of *poblanos rellenos*, or poblano-stuffed peppers?

Chile roasters have become common in the Southwest over the past few years, and these cylindrical cages with gas jets below can roast a forty-pound sack of chile in much less time than it takes to grill each pod. Although it is a more-convenient way to process large quantities of pods, there are some drawbacks to using a roaster. Occasionally, the pods are roasted unevenly, and some are difficult to peel. The pods are usually placed in a large plastic bag to steam after being roasted and must be processed as soon as they have cooled enough to handle. If allowed to sit for too long, bacteria growth can cause the pods to spoil.

Creative chileheads have come up with some unusual methods for taking the skins off chiles. One man wrote to tell me he blistered each pod individually with a small propane torch, and added that the flame can easily be directed into the creases. The most unusual skin removal method was:

"Freeze the fresh chiles solid. Using a dry rag to hold one end of the frozen pepper, use a vegetable peeler to peel the skin off, then a small knife or garnishing tool to scrape in the crevices the peeler missed." Yes, that's a way to remove the skin, and now, you have a naked, raw, and frozen poblano pod with seeds inside instead of a roasted, peeled, and deseeded one with all the enhanced aromas, flavors, and textures that the fire brings—the form called for in many of these recipes.

Freezing Poblano Peppers

Roasted and peeled green poblano pods can be frozen for future use. If they are to be frozen whole (rather than chopped), the pods do not have to be peeled first. In fact, they are easier to peel after they have been frozen. Peel the pods if they are to be frozen in strips or chopped form. A handy way to put up chopped or diced chiles is to freeze them in plastic ice cube trays. After they are frozen, they can be popped out of the trays and stored in a bag. When making a recipe calling for chopped poblano chile, just drop in a cube or two! This method eliminates the problem of trying to break apart a large slab of frozen chopped pods when just a couple of ounces is needed.

Drying Poblanos to Make Anchos

There are three main methods of drying red poblano pods to make anchos: in the sun, in the oven, or in a food dehydrator. The sun method requires a dry climate and hot sun; the fresh pods are placed on trays and covered with cheesecloth to keep insects off. It will take a week or two for the pods to dry and become anchos. A quicker way is using the oven on the lowest possible setting and closely monitor the drying to make sure the pods don't burn. The fresh pods are rather bulky for food dehydrators, but you can always cut them in half lengthwise to make them flatter.

After they are dried but still bendable, double-bag them using zip bags and place them in the freezer. If rehydrated anchos are called for in a recipe, they can be reconstituted in two ways. They can be fried in a little oil until they puff and reconstitute slightly, or they can be soaked in hot water for fifteen to twenty minutes for full rehydration.

Making and Storing Ancho Powder

Although the best whole anchos are those with a little moisture and "bend" to them, they are not dry enough to make into a powder and will gum up your spice mill. To make a powder, remove the seeds and stems and dry the chiles until they break, either in the oven with the setting on the lowest temperature or in a food dehydrator. Then use your spice mill or small blender to grind them into a powder. The proper long-time preservation method to avoid oxidation and spoilage is to tightly pack small bottles full with the powder, screw the top on tightly, and store in the freezer.

PART 3

Anchos and Poblanos in the Kitchen

Culinary Usage

The use of the ancho/poblano, is equally divided between fresh (poblano) and dried (ancho). Approximately half of the Mexican ancho crop is harvested and sold as fresh green chile. These poblano pods are often stuffed with meats and cheeses for *chiles rellenos,* or used in casseroles and sauces much like the New Mexican varieties of the American Southwest. Of the dried ancho crop, about 15 percent is sold as powder and food coloring, with the rest bought in whole pod form and used mostly in sauces, particularly moles. The ancho accounts for approximately one-fifth of all chiles consumed in Mexico.

Salsa Verde Poblana
(Green Poblano Chile Sauce)

This tasty sauce from Chihuahua can be used with enchiladas or, interestingly enough, can be served over pasta, which is very popular in Mexico.

> 6 poblano chiles, roasted, peeled, seeds and stems removed
> 5 serrano chiles, seeds and stems removed
> 1 onion, chopped
> 4 tablespoons butter
> Salt to taste
> 1 cup cream, or more as needed
> 1 cup añejo (aged) cheese, grated, or substitute Romano

In a food processor or blender, combine the chiles and onion, and process into a paste. Heat the butter in a saucepan, and add the chile mixture. Cook for five minutes, stirring well. Season with salt to taste.

Remove the pan from the heat and add the cream and cheese, stirring until completely blended. Add more cream if necessary to adjust to desired consistency. This sauce can be heated gently.

Yield: About 2$\frac{1}{2}$ cups   **Heat scale:** Medium

SALSA DE MOLE POBLANO
(CLASSIC MOLE POBLANO SAUCE)

This subtle blend of chocolate and chile is from Puebla, where it is known as the "National Dish of Mexico" when served over turkey. This sauce adds life to any kind of poultry, from roasted game hens to a simple grilled chicken breast. It is also excellent as a sauce over chicken enchiladas.

4 dried ancho chiles, seeds and stems removed

4 dried red guajillo or New Mexican chiles, seeds and
    stems removed

1 medium onion, chopped

2 cloves garlic, chopped

2 medium tomatoes, peeled and seeds removed, chopped

2 tablespoons sesame seeds

1/2 cup almonds

1/2 corn tortilla, torn into pieces

1/4 cup raisins

1/4 teaspoon ground cloves

1/4 teaspoon ground cinnamon

1/4 teaspoon ground coriander

3 tablespoons shortening or vegetable oil

1 cup chicken broth

1 ounce bitter chocolate (or more to taste)

Combine the chiles, onion, garlic, tomatoes, 1 tablespoon of the sesame seeds, almonds, tortilla, raisins, cloves, cinnamon, and coriander. Puree small amounts of this mixture in a blender until smooth.

Melt the shortening in a skillet and saute the puree for ten minutes, stirring frequently. Add the chicken broth and chocolate, and cook over a very low heat for forty-five minutes. The sauce should be very thick. The remaining sesame seeds are used as a garnish sprinkled over the finished dish.

Yield: 2 cups   **Heat scale:** Medium

ROMESCO SAUCE

Romesco is a classic Spanish sauce that is served with a wide variety of dishes, including the famous *tortilla Española* from the Tarragona region. This classic Catalan sauce combines almonds with two of the most popular horticultural imports from the New World: chiles and tomatoes. The sauce gets its name from the *romesco* chile, but these are not readily available outside Spain. A combination of ancho and New Mexican chiles approximates the flavor.

> 1 ancho chile, stem and seeds removed
> 2 dried red New Mexican red chiles, stems and seeds removed
> 1/2 cup toasted almonds
> 5 cloves garlic, unpeeled
> 2 tomatoes, unpeeled
> 1/2 cup red wine vinegar
> 1/3 cup extra-virgin olive oil, preferably Spanish
> Salt and freshly ground black pepper

Preheat the oven to 200 degrees.

Place the chiles, almonds, garlic, and tomatoes on a baking pan and roast in the oven until the nuts are toasted, the chiles are fragrant, and the skins of the tomatoes and garlic are blistered. The nuts will take about five minutes, the tomatoes about twenty, and the chiles somewhere in between. Check frequently to be sure nothing burns.

Let the ingredients cool. Place the almonds in a spice mill or coffee grinder and process to a powder. Place the chiles in a bowl, cover with hot water, and let them steep for fifteen minutes to soften. Drain the chiles and discard the water. Remove the skins from the tomatoes and garlic.

Put the almonds, chiles, tomatoes, garlic, and vinegar in a blender or food processor, and puree to a smooth paste, adding a little oil if necessary.

Transfer the paste to a bowl and slowly whisk in the oil, 1 teaspoon at a time, until half the oil is absorbed. Gradually add the remaining oil. Season with the salt and pepper.

Let the sauce sit for an hour or two to blend the flavors.

Yield: 1/3 to 1/2 cup   **Heat scale:** Medium

Appetizers
and
Breakfast

POBLANO PEPPER RINGS

Since poblanos make some of the tastiest chiles rellenos, it makes sense that they fry up deliciously. Why not dip these rings in guacamole?

1 cup flour
1 teaspoon salt
1 teaspoon freshly ground black pepper
1/2 teaspoon cayenne powder
3 cups vegetable oil
3 poblano chiles, roasted, peeled, seeds and stems
    removed, cut into quarter-inch rings
1 cup buttermilk

In a bowl, combine the flour, salt, pepper, and cayenne, and mix well. Transfer the mixture to a plate. Heat the oil in a large pan until it just begins to smoke, then lower the heat slightly. Dip the poblano rings in the flour four at a time, shake off any excess, then dip them in the buttermilk and back into the flour. Drop them into the hot oil, and fry until lightly browned. Repeat with the rest of the rings and then drain on paper towels. Serve warm.

Yield: 4 to 6 servings   **Heat scale:** Mild

Scrambled Eggs with Ancho Pork Chorizo

This traditional Mexican sausage is often scrambled with eggs or served with *huevos rancheros* for breakfast. Unlike other sausages, it is usually not placed in a casing but rather served loose or formed into patties. Only a small amount of chorizo is used in this recipe, so freeze the rest in small amounts. Top the scrambled eggs with any of the sauces above. **Note:** This recipe requires advance preparation.

> 1 clove garlic
>
> 1/2 cup ground ancho chile
>
> 1/2 teaspoon freshly ground black pepper
>
> 1/4 teaspoon each: ground cloves, cinnamon,
> oregano, cumin
>
> 1/2 teaspoon salt
>
> 1 teaspoon oregano
>
> 1/2 cup vinegar
>
> 2 pounds ground pork
>
> 3 large eggs, lightly beaten with 2 tablespoons
> half-and-half
>
> Chile sauce of choice

To make the chorizo, combine all the ingredients except the pork, eggs, and half-and-half in a blender and puree. Knead this mixture into the pork until it is thoroughly mixed together. Place in a bowl, cover, and refrigerate for twenty-four hours. To cook, crumble 3/4 cup of the chorizo in a skillet and fry until well-browned. Drain it on paper towels and return it to the skillet. Add the eggs and fry, stirring constantly, until the eggs are set. Serve immediately topped with the sauce.

Yield: 2 servings   **Heat scale:** Medium

CHILE CON QUESO ESTILO SONORA (SONORAN-STYLE CHEESE WITH CHILE)

Who could ask for a more perfect combination than chile and cheese? This recipe is a specialty of the Sonora area, which has millions of acres of agricultural land along the coastal plains. Serve it with tortilla strips or chips for dipping.

1/4 stick butter

1 medium onion, chopped

2 tomatoes, chopped

4 cloves garlic, finely chopped

5 poblano chiles, roasted, peeled, seeds and stems removed, chopped

3 jalapeño chiles, seeds and stems removed, minced

3/4 cup milk

Salt and pepper to taste

1 cup grated Chihuahua cheese or mild cheddar

2 tablespoons chopped cilantro

Melt the butter in a skillet and saute the onion, tomatoes, and garlic until the onions are translucent. Next, add the chiles, milk, salt, and pepper. Let the mixture cook for a few minutes so the flavors blend, then add the cheese, stirring well.

Remove from the heat, place in a glass bowl, and garnish with the cilantro.

Yield: 4 to 6 servings **Heat scale:** Medium

Soups and
Salads

Ensalada de Garbanzos (Chickpea Salad)

Serve this delicious Sonoran-style dish over shredded mixed greens to accompany a fish dish. I recommend using freshly cooked chickpeas, but the canned variety will also work if the peas are thoroughly rinsed. **Note:** This recipe requires advance preparation.

Juice of 1 lemon
Juice of 2 limes
1/4 cup minced cilantro
1/4 cup olive oil
3/4 cup minced onion
2¹/₂ cups cooked chickpeas
6 ounces cream cheese, softened
2 poblano chiles, roasted and peeled, seeds and stems removed, chopped fine
Mixed greens

Mix the citrus juices, cilantro, olive oil, and onion in a medium-sized, nonreactive bowl. Let stand at room temperature for three hours.

In a small bowl, combine the cooked chickpeas, softened cream cheese, and the chiles, and mix thoroughly. Add this to the marinated citrus mixture, and mix thoroughly.

Serve over shredded, mixed greens.

Yield: 4 servings   **Heat scale:** Mild

Caldillo Durangueño (Durango Stew)

A precursor to U.S. chilis con carne, this recipe hails from beautiful, quaint Durango. Serve the *caldillo* or stew on football or soccer days; double the recipe, prepare it the day before, and reheat it. It can simmer for hours, and this only intensifies the flavor. Serve it with warm tortillas or fresh bread, and plenty of cold Mexican beer. **Note:** This recipe requires advance preparation.

    6 poblano chiles, roasted
    2¹/₂ pounds beef roast
    1¹/₂ teaspoons salt
    1/2 pound tomatillos, cut into quarters
    3 cloves garlic, minced
    1 cup chopped onion
    1/2 teaspoon Mexican oregano
    1/2 teaspoon ground cumin
    3 tablespoons chopped cilantro
    3 tablespoons oil

Peel the chiles, and remove the stems and seeds. Place the chiles on wire racks, put the racks on cookie sheets, and place them in a 250-degree oven for one hour.

Place the beef in a shallow pan and sprinkle with the salt. Using a blunt edge, pound the salt into the meat, and let the meat dry out slightly at room temperature for about two hours.

In a pot, heat 3 cups of water to the boiling point and

add the tomatillos, then reduce the heat to a simmer, add the garlic, onion, oregano, cumin, and cilantro, and simmer for thirty minutes, partially covered. Remove from the heat and reserve.

Place the oven-seasoned chiles in a heat-proof bowl, and cover with 1 cup of very hot water. Rehydrate for ten minutes and then drain (reserving the water), dice the chiles, and add them and the reserved water to the cooked tomatillo-onion mixture.

Cut the beef into half-inch cubes; heat the oil in a large, heavy pot, add the beef, and saute for five minutes. Add 3 cups of hot water, bring the mixture to a boil, reduce the heat to a simmer, add half the chile mixture, cover, and simmer for one hour. Then add the remaining chile mixture, cover, and simmer for one hour more. Serve hot.

Yield: 5 servings   **Heat scale:** Mild to medium

VERACRUZ-STYLE SHRIMP CHOWDER

This soup is called *Chilpachole Veracruzano* in Spanish. The use of dried shrimp—available, like the *epazote,* in Latin and Asian markets—intensifies the flavor. There is no substitute for epazote, with its unique, pungent flavor. Serve the shrimp stew in bowls or over cooked rice, and garnish with lemon or lime slices.

8 cloves garlic, unpeeled

2 chipotle chiles, seeds and stems removed

2 ancho chiles, seeds and stems removed

1 onion, cut into eighths

3 tomatoes, peeled and cut into quarters

3 tablespoons vegetable oil

3 cups water or fish stock

8 dried shrimp

1/4 cup epazote

2 pounds fresh shrimp, shelled and deveined

Wrap the unpeeled cloves of garlic in aluminum foil, and roast them in a 400-degree oven for thirty minutes. When they are cool enough to handle, squeeze the garlic out of the skins into a blender.

Using a dry skillet, lightly roast the chiles for two minutes, taking care not to burn them. Add the chiles to the blender along with the onion and the tomatoes, and puree the mixture.

Heat the oil in a medium skillet, pour in the pureed mixture, and cook it over a medium-low heat for one minute.

Then add the water, dried shrimp, and the epazote, and simmer for three minutes.

Add the fresh shrimp and simmer the mixture for an additional five minutes, or until the shrimp are cooked. Add more water if the mixture starts to get too thick. Serve immediately.

Yield: 4 servings   **Heat scale:** Medium

Main Dishes

Mole Coloradito Oaxaqueño (Oaxacan Little Red Mole)

This recipe is from Susana Trilling of Seasons of My Heart cooking school in Oaxaca. She notes that many *señoras* in the small pueblos still insist on using their *molcajetes* for the tedious task of grinding the ingredients for this celebrated dish!

1 whole chicken, cut into eight serving pieces

6 cups chicken stock

5 ancho chiles, stems and seeds removed

2 guajillo chiles, stems and seeds removed, or
   substitute dried red New Mexican chiles

5 whole peppercorns

5 whole cloves

2 cinnamon sticks (each 2 inches long), Mexican preferred

1 white onion, peeled and quartered

10 cloves garlic

3 tablespoons lard or vegetable oil

1 small French roll, sliced

1 small plantain or banana

2 tablespoons raisins

1/4 cup sesame seeds

10 whole almonds

2 medium tomatoes, quartered

3 sprigs fresh marjoram or oregano

1 bar, or to taste, Mexican chocolate, such as Ibarra

1 or 2 avocado leaves or substitute bay leaves

Salt to taste

(continued on next page)

MOLE COLORADITO OAXAQUEÑO (OAXACAN LITTLE RED MOLE)

Simmer the chicken in the stock until tender, about half an hour. Remove the chicken, keep it warm, and reserve the stock.

In a large frying pan or *comal,* toast the chiles, turning once until darkened but not burned. Toast the guajillos a little longer because of their tougher skins. Place the chiles in a bowl and cover with hot water to soak for half an hour to soften. Remove the chiles, place them in a blender or food processor, and puree, adding a little chile water if necessary, then strain.

Toast the peppercorns and cloves lightly in a dry pan or comal. Cool and grind in a molcajete or spice grinder. In the same pan, roast the onions and garlic cloves until slightly browned. Cool and place in a blender or food processor, and puree with a little water.

Heat a tablespoon of the lard in the pan until smoking hot, and fry the bread until lightly brown; remove and drain on paper towels. Fry the plantain on both sides until browned; remove and drain. Quickly fry the raisins, then remove. Lower the heat and add the sesame seeds, stirring constantly for a couple of minutes, then add the almonds and continue to fry until both are well browned. Remove, drain, and combine with the bread, plantain, and raisins, reserving a bit of the sesame seeds for garnish. Place in a blender or food processor and puree, adding a little water if necessary.

Wipe out the skillet with a cloth and add 1 tablespoon lard. When hot, add the tomatoes and fry well. Place in a blender or food processor and puree until smooth, then remove.

Heat a tablespoon of lard in a *cazuela* or heavy pot until smoking. Add the chile puree and fry, stirring constantly so it will not burn. It tends to splatter about, so be careful! Fry for a couple of minutes, add the tomato puree, the ground spices, and the marjoram, and heat through. Stir in the bread mixture and continue to heat, stirring constantly. Add the chocolate and avocado leaves, thin with the reserved chicken stock, and continue to simmer for thirty minutes.

Add the chicken, adjust the salt, and heat through. Serve with black beans, rice, and tortillas.

Yield: 4 to 6 servings   **Heat scale:** Medium

Chiles à la Norita
(Stuffed Ancho Chiles)

Ancho chiles make some of the best stuffed dishes that can be found. However, be careful to choose anchos that are fairly fresh. Look for chiles that are still bendable and have a prevalent aroma through their packaging. Serve with Mexican-style rice and guacamole.

Salsa:

1/4 cup vegetable oil

2 onions, finely chopped

2 green tomatoes, finely chopped

1/2 cup water

1/4 teaspoon Mexican oregano

2 tablespoon cilantro, chopped

Stuffed Chiles:

4 cups water

6 large ancho chiles, stems and seeds removed

13 ounces of aged cheese, such as Romano, sliced into
    6 equal pieces

5 tablespoons butter

1/3 cup vegetable oil

6 tortillas

6 eggs, scrambled

1 head lettuce, shredded or chopped

1 avocado, sliced

7 ounces cheddar cheese, grated

To prepare the salsa, heat the oil in a saucepan and fry the onion. Then add the tomatoes, water, oregano, and cilantro. Leave the mixture on high heat until the tomatoes are fully cooked, then set aside.

To prepare the chiles, boil the water in a large sauce pan, then put the chiles in the boiling water for ten minutes to rehydrate them. Drain the chiles, and carefully pat them dry on paper towels.

Fill the chiles with a slice of cheese and set aside. In a large skillet, melt the butter over medium heat, then add the oil and turn the heat on high. Brown the chiles in the butter/oil mixture. Then remove them from the oil, drain them on a paper towel, and place them on a platter.

Briefly dip the tortillas in the oil, and place them on a separate plate. Place one chile on top of each tortilla, then top them with a spoonful of salsa and egg.

Decorate the plates with the lettuce, avocado slices, and shredded cheese.

Yield: 4 to 6 servings   **Heat scale:** Medium

Poblanos Rellenos con Res y Pasa (Beef- and Raisin-Stuffed Poblanos)

This stuffed chile recipe is from Aguascalientes, which translates as hot water since the town is close to thermal springs. The recipe is unusual in that the chiles are not battered and fried. Thus, the pure taste of roasted chiles shines through.

> 1 pound beef roast
> 1 clove garlic, chopped
> 1/2 teaspoon salt
> 1/2 onion, chopped
> 1 tablespoon vegetable oil
> 1 cup chopped tomato
> 1 tablespoon vinegar
> 10 olives, chopped
> 20 raisins, chopped
> 10 almonds, peeled and chopped
> 6 poblano chiles, roasted, peeled, seeds removed
> 1/2 cup cream
> 1/2 cup grated Mexican cheese of choice
> Cilantro leaves for garnish

Add garlic and salt to water covering the meat in a large pot, and simmer for about an hour. Once the meat is cooked, remove it from the pot and chop it into small pieces.

Heat the oil in a skillet, and saute the onion until soft. Add the tomato and vinegar, and fry a while longer. Then add the meat and stir. Add the olives, raisins, almonds, and salt to taste. Stuff the chiles with this mixture, and place in the oven on a greased cookie sheet. Bake at 350 degrees for ten minutes. Heat the cream and cheese in a pan and drizzle the mixture evenly over each chile as it is served. Garnish with the cilantro leaves.

Yield: 6 servings   **Heat scale:** Mild

Almendrado Oaxaqueño
(Almond Chicken Oaxacan-Style)

The Oaxaca marketplace is famous for its incredible selection of chiles and other locally grown produce. This is one of the signature dishes using ingredients found in the market.

1 medium chicken, sectioned

Salt and pepper to taste

Corn oil as needed for frying

3 ancho chiles, stems and seeds removed

1/2 cup almonds

4 tomatoes, roasted, peeled, and seeded

2 cloves garlic

1 medium onion

6 black peppercorns

3 cloves

1 cinnamon stick

1/2 bolillo (or small French roll), in crumbs

2 tablespoons sugar

4 cups chicken broth

In a large skillet, salt and pepper the chicken and fry it in the oil, making sure it doesn't burn or stick, then remove the chicken from the pan and drain.

In the same grease, fry the chiles, all but two tablespoons of the almonds, tomatoes, garlic, onion, peppercorns, cloves, cinnamon, and bread crumbs. Pour the mixture into a blender and blend until smooth. If necessary, add a little broth. Return the mixture to the pan and cook at a low temperature. Add the chicken, sugar, and chicken broth. Cover and cook at a low temperature until the chicken is tender. Before serving, add the remaining almonds.

Yield: 4 to 6 servings   **Heat scale:** Medium

Barbacoa de Langostinos (Barbecued Langostinos)

This is a beautifully spiced way of serving langostinos! Because the lobster is so rich, serve the dish with simple but elegant side dishes, such as a tomato salad with Balsamic vinegar dressing and maybe some good pasta. A citrus dessert would be the perfect touch. The authentic touch in this recipe is to serve the langostinos and chile sauce as they do in Veracruz—on banana leaves.

  4 ancho chiles, seeds and stems removed
  3 pasilla chiles, seeds and stems removed
  6 tablespoons corn or canola oil
  1/2 teaspoon salt
  3 cups peeled, coarsely chopped tomatoes
  10 cloves garlic, minced
  1 cup chopped onion
  1/2 teaspoon ground black pepper
  2 whole cloves, ground
  1/4 teaspoon cinnamon
  1/2 teaspoon cumin
  1/4 teaspoon freshly ground black pepper
  2 tablespoons white wine vinegar
  2 pounds cleaned langostinos, split lengthwise
     (or substitute lobster tails)

Tear the chile into strips and cover with one cup boiling water. Soak for ten minutes, then put the chiles and soaking water into a blender, puree, and set aside.

Heat three tablespoons of the oil in a medium skillet and saute the tomatoes, salt, half of the minced garlic, onion, half the ground black pepper, half the ground cloves, cinnamon, cumin, and the pureed chile mixture. Then simmer, covered, for fifteen minutes. Remove from the heat and reserve.

In a small bowl, mix the remaining garlic, ground cloves, 1/4 teaspoon black pepper, and the vinegar. Set aside.

Cook the langostinos in a pot of boiling water for eight minutes. Drain and plunge them into cold water to cool them quickly, then drain and remove the meat and cube it. Toss the meat in the reserved bowl of the garlic-vinegar mixture.

Heat the remaining three tablespoons of oil in a saute pan, add the langostino mixture, and saute for thirty seconds. Then add the reserved chile mixture and bring to a boil. Quickly reduce the heat, cover, and simmer for five minutes, or until it is hot. Serve immediately.

Yield: 3 to 4 servings **Heat scale:** Mild

Chiles Anchos Encaramelados con Picadillo en Salsa de Aguacate (Caramelized Ancho Chiles with Picadillo in Avocado Sauce)

"This is one of my top creations regarding chiles," says Mexico City chef Lula Bertrán. "The key to this recipe is the absorption of the orange juice into the skin of the ancho, making the chile soft enough to eat. Make sure you choose anchos that are still pliable; if they are hard as a brick, they will need to be steamed first." The presentation of the chiles is elegant on the light green sauce.

THE CHILES:
6 medium ancho chiles, stems left on

1 quart water

1 1/2 cups orange juice

1/2 cup grated piloncillo (raw sugar), or substitute molasses

1/2 cup vinegar

1 teaspoon salt

THE PICADILLO:
3 tablespoons vegetable oil

1 clove garlic, minced

1 small onion, chopped fine

1/2 pound ground beef

1/2 pound ground pork

1/4 cup raisins

1 medium tomato, chopped

2 teaspoons minced cilantro

5 serrano chiles, seeds and stems removed, minced

1/2 teaspoon Mexican oregano

Salt to taste

AVOCADO SAUCE:

3 tomatillos, husks removed

2 tablespoons chopped onion

2 serrano chiles, seeds and stems removed, halved

1 clove garlic

1 tablespoon chopped cilantro

1 avocado, peeled

1 teaspoon lime juice

1/8 teaspoon sugar

1/2 teaspoon salt

1/2 cup half-and-half

Take each ancho by the stem and use a scissors to cut a T-shaped incision across the shoulders of the chile and about two-thirds down the pod. Carefully remove the seeds and membrane. In a pan, bring the quart of water to the boiling point. Add the cleaned anchos and cook at a low boil for fifteen minutes, turning once (carefully). Remove from the heat and let cool. Then remove the anchos, clean off any remaining seeds, and drain on paper towels.

(continued on next page)

CHILES ANCHOS ENCARAMELADOS CON PICADILLO EN SALSA DE AGUACATE (CARAMELIZED ANCHO CHILES WITH PICADILLO IN AVOCADO SAUCE)

To make the picadillo, heat the oil, and saute the onion and garlic. Add the beef and pork, turn the heat to high, and brown thoroughly, stirring often. Drain nearly all the fat and liquid from the meat mixture. Add the remaining ingredients, and cook uncovered over medium heat for about fifteen to twenty minutes.

To make the sauce, combine all the ingredients in a food processor and puree. Add half-and-half if necessary; the sauce should be just thin enough to pour. Strain it, and heat in a saucepan, but do not boil.

To assemble the dish, carefully stuff the anchos, and place each one on a plate. Heat the plates in the oven or a microwave. Drizzle the sauce over each ancho, add the side dishes, and serve.

Yield: 6 servings   **Heat scale:** Medium

Filete en Salsa de Oregano (Fillet in Oregano Sauce)

From Sinaloa, this recipe features oregano, a member of the mint family. Mexican oregano offers a much stronger flavor than Italian or Mediterranean oregano, so remember that a little goes a long way!

    2 pounds beef medallions
    2 tablespoons butter
    3 tablespoons oil
    2 cups fresh Mexican oregano leaves, ground
    1 cup chicken broth
    1 poblano chile, roasted, peeled, stem and seeds removed
    1 cup cream
    2 tablespoons minced onion
    Salt and pepper to taste
    Fresh Mexican oregano leaves for garnish

Heat one tablespoon butter and the oil in a skillet, and cook the beef to taste. Set aside and keep warm.

In a blender, combine the oregano leaves with the broth, chile, cream, and onion, and puree. Strain the mixture, then heat the remaining butter and cook the sauce for about twenty-five minutes, adding salt and pepper to taste, stirring constantly.

Serve the sauce over the medallions and decorate with oregano leaves.

Yield: 6 servings   **Heat scale:** Mild

Smoked Pork Mole Enchiladas

Serve these unusual enchiladas with a chilled citrus salad, rice pilaf, and a seasoned green vegetable dish.

2 ancho chiles, stems and seeds removed
2 pasilla chiles, stems and seeds removed
3 dried red New Mexican chiles, stems and seeds removed
3 cups water
2 cups chicken broth
1 large onion, chopped
1 pork roast (4- to 6-pounds)
1 dozen corn tortillas
2 tablespoons vegetable oil
1 cup sour cream
1 cup commercial mole sauce
1/4 cup sesame seeds

Simmer the chiles in the water for fifteen minutes to soften. Place the chiles, onion, and the chicken broth in a blender and puree until smooth. Strain the sauce if desired.

Make diagonal slits about one-inch deep in the pork roast. Rub the chile mixture over the roast, penetrating deeply into the cuts.

Smoke the roast in a smoker with indirect heat, following the directions provided by the manufacturer. When the roast is done, after smoking to an internal temperature of 160 degrees, carve it into thin strips.

Soften the tortillas by frying them in oil in a small skillet for a few seconds on each side, then drain them on paper towels. Place the pork strips in the tortillas, top with sour cream and sesame seeds, and roll up. Place them in a baking dish, cover with mole sauce, and bake in a 325-degree oven for about twenty minutes. Sprinkle the sesame seeds on top and serve.

Yield: 6 to 8 servings   **Heat scale:** Medium

Chilorio Sorpresa (Pork Surprise)

The pork comes out surprisingly tender in this excellent recipe from Playa del Carmen. The Maya used wild boar for this dish until the Spanish introduced domesticated pigs.

2 pounds pork meat, cubed
Water as needed
1 tablespoon salt
1 cup orange juice
6 ancho chiles, stems and seeds removed
1 pasilla chile, stems and seeds removed
5 cloves garlic
1 small onion, chopped
1 teaspoon oregano powder
1/4 teaspoon cumin powder
1 teaspoon black pepper
1/4 cup vinegar
1/2 cup beef broth
2 tablespoons pork lard, or substitute shortening
1 small onion, sliced
2 squash, sliced and lightly boiled

Place the meat in a skillet with a little water, salt, and orange juice, and cook, covered, until the meat is tender, about forty-five minutes, then shred and set aside.

Place the chiles, garlic, onion, oregano, cumin, pepper, vinegar, and beef broth in a blender and blend until smooth, then set aside.

In a separate skillet, heat the lard and fry the meat and chile mixture together until blended. Serve with the onion and squash.

Yield: 6 to 8 servings   **Heat scale:** Medium

CAMARONES EN CHILE ROJO
(SHRIMP IN RED CHILE)

The ancho chiles in this recipe from the State of México do not overpower the delicate flavor of the shrimp; instead, they add just a bit of heat and color. Serve this dish with warm tortillas, a chopped lettuce and tomato salad, and minted fresh fruit for dessert.

6 ancho chiles, stems and seeds removed

Water for soaking

2 cloves garlic

1 medium onion, coarsely chopped

3 medium tomatoes

2 tablespoons vegetable oil

Water for shrimp

1/2 teaspoon salt

1/4 teaspoon freshly ground black pepper

1 pound fresh whole shrimp

1/4 cup coarsely chopped epazote

2 potatoes, peeled and cut in small cubes

Toast the chiles in a hot dry skillet for one minute, tossing constantly so they don't burn. Place the chiles in a heat-resistant bowl, cover with water, and soak for fifteen minutes. Then drain the chiles and reserve the water.

Put the drained chiles in a small blender with the garlic and onion, and puree the ingredients, adding more of the soaking water if necessary. Set the mixture aside.

Roast the tomatoes by holding them over a gas flame

until they blister, or gently roll them in a small, dry saute pan until they start to blister. Remove the skins, crush them between your fingers, and add them to the heated vegetable oil in a saute pan. Saute the tomatoes for thirty seconds, and then add the reserved chile mixture and saute for thirty seconds more; remove the pan from the heat and reserve.

Wash the shrimp, place them in a small saucepan, cover with water, and add the salt, pepper, and epazote. Bring the water to a boil, reduce the heat to a simmer, and cook for two minutes. Remove the shrimp from the water, and when they are cool enough to handle, clean them and cut in half lengthwise. Reserve the cooking water.

Cook the potatoes in the shrimp water for ten minutes, or until they are tender. Reserve one cup of the water, and then drain the potatoes. Add the sliced shrimp and the potatoes to the chile mixture, and toss to blend. Then heat and serve.

Yield: 3 servings   **Heat scale:** Mild

CABRITO Y RES CON CHILES ANCHOS
(BRAISED GOAT AND BEEF WITH ANCHO CHILES)

Goat is often saved for celebrations in Mexico, such as a baptism or wedding. The baby goats, or kids as they are called, offer the most tender, succulent meat imaginable. This recipe from Nayarít includes beef and is flavored with ancho chiles. Lamb may be substituted for the goat.

> 5 ancho chiles, toasted, stems and seeds removed,
>   rehydrated
> 2 pounds tomatoes, chopped
> 1 pinch ginger
> 8 black peppercorns
> 5 cloves garlic
> 1/2 teaspoon cumin
> 2 cloves
> 1/2 cup vinegar
> 1/2 cup dry red wine
> 2 bay leaves
> 2 pounds goat or lamb meat, cut into 1-inch cubes
> 2 pounds beef, cut into 1-inch cubes
> Tortillas

In a food processor or blender, combine the chiles, tomatoes, ginger, peppercorns, garlic, cumin, cloves, and vinegar, and puree in batches. Remove to a bowl, and add the wine and bay leaves. Place the goat and beef in a large baking pan, and pour the chile mixture over it. Bake covered at 250 degrees for two hours, or until done and the meat is falling apart.

Serve with tortillas and the salsa of your choice.

Yield: 8 to 10 servings   **Heat scale:** Mild to medium

CARNITAS CON CHILE NEGRO
(STEAK WITH BLACK CHILE)

This recipe features a variety of poblano that is grown exclusively in Queréndaro, Michoacán. These Morelia pods dry to a dark black color, thus are called *chile negro*. If they are unavailable, substitute the darkest poblano chiles. Serve over green rice.

6 green tomatoes, roasted
10 chiles negros, roasted, peeled, stems and seeds
    removed (reserve the seeds)
2 cloves garlic
1/4 cup olive oil
2 pounds flank steak, cut into 1/2-inch cubes
1/2 cup chopped cilantro
1 pinch cumin
Salt to taste
Tortillas

In a blender, combine the tomatoes, chiles, and garlic, and process until coarsely chopped. Heat the olive oil in a skillet, then fry the tomato mixture for about ten minutes, stirring constant. Add the meat, cilantro, cumin, and salt, and simmer for thirty minutes. Serve, decorated with the seeds, with tortillas on the side.

Yield: 4 to 6 servings   **Heat scale:** Medium

Side Dishes

Arroz con Chiles Poblanos Rojos (Rice with Red Poblano Chiles)

This rice recipe from Nuevo León in Mexico is unusual because of the addition of green tomatoes (or tomatillos) and sliced hard-boiled eggs. The roasted red poblano chile adds the color and a dash of heat. Serve the rice with a chicken dish or with any of the moles in this book.

3 tablespoons olive oil
2 cups rice
1 cup minced onion
2 cloves garlic, minced
2 jalapeño chiles, seeds and stems removed,
     cut into thin rings
1 cup chopped tomatillos, or substitute green tomatoes
1/2 teaspoon ground cumin
1/2 teaspoon salt
1/4 teaspoon freshly ground black pepper
4 cups beef stock
2 red poblano chiles, roasted, peeled, chopped fine
2 hard-boiled eggs, sliced

Heat the oil in a medium saucepan, and saute the rice, onion, garlic, jalapeño chiles, tomatillos, cumin, salt, and black pepper for two minutes or until the rice turns golden. Stir in the broth, bring the mixture to a boil, cover, and reduce the heat. Cook the rice for twenty to thirty minutes.

Stir in the red poblano chiles and the eggs, and serve.

Yield: 4 to 6 servings   **Heat scale:** Medium

Tacos Rellenos de Camarón (Shrimp Tacos)

Since fresh shrimp is found in abundance, shrimp tacos are popular with locals and tourists alike on all coasts of Mexico. They are sold as street food as well as appearing on menus at the finest restaurants. Here is a particularly tasty taco treat from Campeche.

5 ancho chiles, seeds and stems removed, rehydrated in hot water
2 tomatoes, peeled and deseeded
1 onion, chopped
1/4 teaspoon salt
Corn oil, as needed to fry tortillas
18 tortillas
2 tablespoons olive oil
2 cups finely chopped shrimp
2 tomatoes, crushed
1 onion, finely chopped
1 habanero chile, seeds and stems removed, minced
1½ cups finely chopped, cooked potatoes
1/2 teaspoon salt
Freshly ground black pepper to taste
2 cups thinly sliced onion, soaked in 1/2 cup vinegar
5 cups finely shredded lettuce

Place the ancho chiles, tomatoes, onion, and salt in a food processor, and process until the mixture is a smooth puree. Set the mixture aside.

Heat the corn oil in a deep-sided skillet. Dip each tortilla in the ancho chile mixture, then fry for a few seconds on each side, draining on paper towels. Place the tortillas on a platter.

Heat the two tablespoons of olive oil in a medium skillet, and add the shrimp, tomatoes, finely chopped onion, habanero chile, and potatoes. Lightly fry the mixture for two minutes, until the shrimp is cooked. Add the salt and pepper to taste. Stuff this mixture into the tortillas and roll up each one.

Drain the onion-vinegar mixture thoroughly and sprinkle it over the tortillas, along with the shredded lettuce.

Yield: 6 servings   **Heat scale:** Medium to hot

CALABACITAS EN ADOBILLO
(SQUASH IN ADOBO SAUCE)

When you eat chayote squash, you are eating a part of history, starting with the Aztecs and the Mayas. Chayote was one of the mainstays of their diet. The squash has a delicate taste and takes well to high seasoning. This side dish from Sinaloa goes well with any meat, poultry, or seafood dish.

    2 ancho chiles, seeds and stems removed
    Hot water
    3 garlic cloves
    1 teaspoon dried thyme
    1/4 teaspoon ground cumin
    1/2 teaspoon salt
    2 teaspoons butter or oil
    1/4 cup chopped onion
    3 tablespoons dried bread crumbs
    2 tablespoons cider vinegar
    1 pound chayote squash, peeled and sliced into
        1/4-inch slices

Tear the ancho chile into strips, put them into a small dish, add one cup of hot water, and let the chile rehydrate for twenty minutes.

Pour the chiles and water into a blender, add the garlic, thyme, cumin, and salt, and puree until smooth. Set aside.

Heat the butter in a skillet, and saute the onion for one minute. Add the chile puree along with the bread crumbs and cider vinegar, cover, and simmer for ten minutes. Stir the mixture, and add more water or stock if it gets too thick.

While the sauce is simmering, steam the chayote squash in half a cup of water for eight minutes. Drain and then add to the simmering sauce. Serve immediately.

Yield: 5 to 6 servings   **Heat scale:** Mild

Rajas con Crema
(Sliced Chiles with Cream)

This is a rich accompaniment from Jalisco, an area rich in its food and traditions which includes Guadalajara, one of the most famous cities in Mexico. My wife, Mary Jane, ate in a large restaurant there that specialized in *cabrito* (goat), and the waiters wore roller skates! Serve this classy dish over hot, cooked rice, and for the entree, serve a simple, spicy grilled fish dish.

> 8 poblano chiles, roasted, peeled, and seeds and
>   stems removed
> 3 tablespoons butter
> 3 tablespoons oil
> 3 cups thinly sliced onion
> 1/2 teaspoon salt
> 1/4 teaspoon freshly ground black or white pepper
> 2 to 2 1/2 cups chicken stock
> 3/4 cup cream
> 1/4 pound grated asadero cheese, or substitute
>   queso blanco or Monterey Jack cheese

Slice the poblano chiles into strips, and set aside.

Heat the butter and oil in a medium-size saute pan, and add the onions; sprinkle with the salt and pepper, and saute the onions for three minutes, or until they are just beginning to brown.

Stir in the reserved chile strips, and toss the mixture over low heat for one minute.

Add 2 cups of the chicken stock and the cream to the onion-chile saute; bring the mixture to a light boil, and reduce the heat immediately to a simmer. Stir the mixture frequently until it starts to thicken slightly, about one minute. If it thickens too much too fast, add a few tablespoons of the chicken stock.

Sprinkle the cheese, and gently combine it with the simmering mixture. Serve immediately over hot, cooked rice.

Yield: 4 to 5 servings   **Heat scale:** Mild

Frijoles Charros (Cowboy Beans)

Here is the classic recipe from Sonora, Cowboy Beans. The *chicharrón* in this recipe is fried pork cracklings, and can be seasoned with different sauces and seasonings, depending on the region. In the U.S., they can be purchased in many groceries, since former President George H.W. Bush made them famous as his favorite snack! **Note:** This recipe requires advance preparation.

> 1 pound cleaned pinto beans
> 2 cups beer, not dark
> 3 tablespoons vegetable oil
> 1 pound cooked pork, shredded
> 1/4 cup ground ancho chiles
> 2 cups hot commercial salsa of choice
> 3/4 cup chicharrón

Place the beans in a large, heavy casserole pot, cover with cold water, and boil for two minutes. Turn off the heat, and allow the beans to sit for one hour. Drain the beans and return them to the cleaned casserole, add the beer, and enough hot water to cover, going about two inches above the beans. Bring the mixture to a boil, reduce the heat to a simmer, and partially cover.

Heat the oil in a skillet, and saute the shredded pork, ancho chiles, and salsa, and simmer for one minute. Stir this sauteed mixture into the cooking beans, cover, and simmer for three to three and a half hours, stirring occasionally and adding more water if the beans get too dry. You want a semi-soupy consistency.

Just before serving, stir the chicharrón into the beans.

Yield: 6 servings   **Heat scale:** Medium

Drinks, Breads, and Desserts

Ancho-Flavored Vodka

When I write "flavored," I mean it, as I have chosen the chiles that impart the most distinct flavors. The raisiny flavor of the ancho melds with the apricot overtones of the habanero and the earthiness of the New Mexican chile to create a finely tuned, fiery, sipping vodka. Of course, use an excellent vodka like Stolichnaya or Absolut. **Note:** This recipe requires advance preparation.

> 1 liter vodka
>
> 1 ancho chile, seeds and stems removed, cut into thin strips
>
> 1/2 dried red New Mexican chile pod, seeds and stems removed, cut in fourths
>
> 1/4 habanero chile, seeds and stems removed, left whole

Open the bottle of vodka and drink some of it to make room in the bottle. Add the chiles and recap. Let sit for at least three days to generate some heat, and the vodka will get progressively hotter over the weeks. As you drink it, replace it with more fresh vodka, and the process will go on for some time.

Yield: About 1 liter   **Heat scale:** Varies but is best served with medium heat

Ancho Chile and Rum-Mulled Citrus Cider

To "mull" a beverage is to heat it with other ingredients to impart a flavor. I mulled over several formulas before choosing this one with its pungent punch.

2 quarts apple cider
1 tablespoon finely ground ancho or pasilla chile
1 lemon, sliced very thin
1/2 orange, sliced very thin
2 teaspoons lemon juice
4 cinnamon sticks (3 inches each)
2 tablespoons whole cloves
2 cups dark rum

Combine all the ingredients in a large saucepan and heat, but do not bring to a boil. Simmer on low heat for fifteen minutes. Strain the mixture through a sieve, pour into mugs, and serve warm.

Yield: 6 to 8 servings   **Heat scale:** Mild

ANCHO-CHOCOLATE MOUSSE WITH GRAND MARNIER

Ah, there's nothing like a *mousse* to complete a dinner, and this one is spiked with the raisiny flavors of ancho chile. You can use other chiles, but only pasilla powder has flavor similar to ancho.

> 1 package sweet baking chocolate (4 ounces)
> 4 squares semisweet chocolate (1 ounce each)
> 1/4 cup Grand Marnier or other orange-flavored liqueur
> 1 teaspoon ancho chile powder, freshly ground if possible
> 2 cups whipping cream
> 1/2 cup sifted powered sugar
> Semisweet chocolate curls for garnish

Combine the chocolates, Grand Marnier, and ancho powder in a heavy saucepan, and cook over low heat until the chocolate melts, stirring constantly. Remove from the heat, and cool to lukewarm.

Beat the whipping cream, adding the powered sugar, until soft peaks form. Gently fold in the whipped cream. Spoon the mousse into individual serving dishes, and chill until ready to serve. Garnish with semisweet chocolate curls removed with a potato peeler.

Yield: 6 servings   **Heat scale:** Mild

ANCHO-PIQUIN SPOONBREAD

This spicy spoonbread recipe combines anchos (for their raisiny flavor) and piquins (for their heat). It is an ideal breakfast bread when combined with a spicy fruit jam.

    2 tablespoons vegetable oil
    1/4 cup diced green bell peppers
    1 small onion, minced
    2 pounds tomatoes, peeled and diced (not drained), or
        substitute 1 can of tomatoes (28 ounces)
    1 cup cornmeal
    1 egg
    2 teaspoons ancho chile powder
    1/2 teaspoon piquin chile powder
    1/2 teaspoon baking soda
    1/2 teaspoon salt
    1 cup shredded Monterey Jack cheese
    Milk as needed

Preheat the oven to 350 degrees.

Heat the oil in a skillet, and saute the green bell peppers and the onion for two minutes. Add the tomatoes to the mixture, and saute on low heat for ten minutes. Transfer to a bowl and mix in the cornmeal, egg, chile powders, baking soda, salt, and cheese, and mix thoroughly. If the mixture seems extremely thick, add milk (by tablespoons) until it is thick but pourable. Pour into a well-greased 1$^1/_2$-quart casserole. Bake for one hour or until firm. Serve hot.

Yield: 4 to 6 servings   **Heat scale:** Medium

Strawberry-Ancho Blue Corn Muffins

Sure, these muffins are great for breakfast when served with fresh mangos dusted with red chile powder, or even a granola cereal, but they can also be served as dessert with ice cream or sorbet.

1 cup flour

3/4 cup blue corn meal

1/3 cup sugar

3 teaspoons baking powder

3/4 teaspoon salt

2 teaspoons ancho chile powder

1 cup finely chopped strawberries

1 cup milk

1 egg beaten

2 tablespoons melted butter

Preheat the oven to 425 degrees.

Sift all the dry ingredients together in a bowl. In a separate bowl, combine the strawberries, milk, egg, and butter. Pour the dry ingredients into the wet ones, and mix well.

Lightly grease a muffin pan, and pour the batter into the cups, about half full. Bake for fifteen to twenty minutes.

Yield: 12 to 15 muffins   **Heat scale:** Medium

Coconut Ginger Flan with Ancho

This recipe is adapted from Susana Trilling, who owns the Seasons of My Heart Cooking School at Rancho Aurora in Oaxaca. She wrote in *Chile Pepper* magazine: "This is one of the favorite desserts of my students at Rancho Aurora. It's much better to make it a day ahead and chill it icy cold."

- 1/4 cup plus 3 tablespoons sugar
- 1/2 cup sliced almonds
- 2 cans coconut milk—not sweetened coconut syrup— (12 ounces each)
- 1/2 cup milk
- 6 eggs
- 5 egg yolks
- 1/4 teaspoon vanilla extract
- 1 teaspoon ancho chile powder (freshly ground preferred)
- 1 tablespoon minced crystallized ginger

Preheat the oven to 350 degrees.

In a saute pan, melt the 3 tablespoons of sugar over medium heat until brown and bubbly; do not stir. Remove and pour into a *flan* pan (a round, nine-inch pan), and rotate the pan so the sugar syrup completely covers the bottom. Place the almonds on the syrup, and set the pan aside.

Combine the coconut milk, sugar, milk, eggs, egg yolks, vanilla, and ancho powder, and whisk well. Add the ginger, stir well, and pour the mixture into the pan.

Place the pan in a water bath, cover with aluminum foil, and bake for one hour. Remove from the oven and chill.

To serve, flip the pan over on a platter, garnish with more ginger; thinly slice.

Yield: 6 servings   **Heat scale:** Mild

PART 4

Resources

Further Reading

• DeWitt, Dave and Paul W. Bosland. *The Complete Chile Pepper Book: Choosing, Growing, Preserving, and Cooking.* Portland, OR: Timber Press, 2009.

• DeWitt, Dave. *1001 Best Hot & Spicy Recipes.* Chicago: Surrey Books, 2010.

• DeWitt, Dave. *The Southwest Table: Traditional Foods from Texas, New Mexico, and Arizona.* New York: Lyons Press, 2011.

• DeWitt, Dave. *Dave DeWitt's Chile Trivia.* Albuquerque: Sunbelt Media, 2012.

Seed and Plant Sources

For seeds, go to the Chile Pepper Institute, **www.chile pepperinstitute.org**, Paul W. Bosland, publisher; Danise Coon, editor.

For five hundred varieties of chile pepper bedding plants in season and fresh chile pods in the late summer and early fall, go to Cross Country Nurseries, **www.chileplants.com**, Janie Lamson, publisher.

Websites

For detailed information on chile peppers around the world:

• The Fiery Foods and Barbecue SuperSite, **www.fiery-foods.com**, Dave DeWitt, publisher; Lois Manno, editor. This site has more than four hundred articles on chile varieties, gardening, history, cooking, and Q&As.

• The Chileman, **www.thechileman.org**, Mark McMillan, publisher and editor. This U.K. site contains the best glossary of chile pepper varieties, with about four thousand listed.

• Pepperworld.com, **www.pepperworld.com** (German language), Harald Zoschke, publisher and editor. The site's many articles include European chile-growing information.

• The Chile Pepper Institute, **www.chilepepperinstitute.org**, Paul W. Bosland, publisher and director; Danise Coon, editor and assistant director. The shop at this site contains books, chile information, and the seeds for dozens of chile varieties.

• Fatalii.net, **www.fatalii.net**, a Finnish site, in English, with extensive information about chile growing and bonsai chiles. Jukka Kilpinnen is the publisher and editor.

• The Burn! Blog, **www.burn-blog.com**, which keeps chileheads and BBQ freaks in touch with the latest news, personalities, and weirdness in the worlds of chile peppers, spiced-up foods, and barbecues

CHILE PEPPER SUPPLIERS AND ONLINE HOTSHOPS

MexGrocer, **www.MexGrocer.com**, has many varieties of worldwide chiles as dried pods and powders.

Melissa's/World Variety Produce, Inc., **www.melissas.com**, has worldwide fresh chiles in season, as well as a fine collection of dried pods and powders.

Peppers, **www.peppers.com**, has the best selection of chile pepper and barbecue products such as hot sauces, salsas, jams, cookies, candies, rubs, chili mixes—the list is very long.

ABOUT THE AUTHOR

I f Dave DeWitt's life were a menu, it would feature dishes as diverse as alligator stew and apple pie à la mode—not to mention the beloved chile peppers that have become the basic ingredient of so many of his projects and accomplishments.

Since starting out in the electronic media, Dave has built careers as a businessman, educator, administrator, producer, on-camera personality, author, and publisher. Currently, in addition to serving as CEO of Sunbelt Shows and co-producer of the National Fiery Foods & Barbecue Show, Dave is always busy sharing his chile pepper expertise in as wide a range of forums as possible.

Besides writing more than forty books (mostly on fiery foods but also including novels, food histories, and travel guides), Dave is publisher of the Fiery Foods & BBQ Super Site (at **www.fiery-foods.com**), and was a founder of Chile Pepper magazine and Fiery Foods & Barbecue magazine.

From his beginning as a radio announcer, Dave went on to own audio/video production companies for which he wrote, produced, and voiced hundreds of radio and television commercials. After moving to New Mexico in 1974, he wrote and hosted the "Captain Space" TV show which beat out both "Saturday Night Live" and "Star Trek" in its Saturday midnight time slot, and, in an entirely different sphere, curated the Albuquerque Museum's 1984 exhibit *Edward S. Curtis in New Mexico.*

The interest in chile peppers and spicy foods that has helped make Dave one of the foremost authorities in the world has led to such best-sellers as *The Whole Chile Pepper Book*, *The Pepper Garden*, *The Hot Sauce Bible*, *The Chile Pepper Encyclopedia*, and *The Spicy Food Lover's Bible*. His latest book on the subject is *Chile Trivia*. As the ultimate testament to his fame and achievement, *The New York Times* has declared him to be "the Pope of Peppers."

Dave is an associate professor in Consumer and Environmental Sciences on the adjunct faculty of New Mexico State University, and also serves as chair of the Board of Regents of the New Mexico Farm and Ranch Heritage Museum.